Arms & Hands

Julie Murray

Abdo
YOUR BODY
Kids

abdopublishing.com

Published by Abdo Kids, a division of ABDO, PO Box 398166, Minneapolis, Minnesota 55439.
Copyright © 2016 by Abdo Consulting Group, Inc. International copyrights reserved in all countries.
No part of this book may be reproduced in any form without written permission from the publisher.

Printed in the United States of America, North Mankato, Minnesota.

102015

012016

THIS BOOK CONTAINS
RECYCLED MATERIALS

Photo Credits: iStock, Shutterstock

Production Contributors: Teddy Borth, Jennie Forsberg, Grace Hansen

Design Contributors: Candice Keimig, Dorothy Toth

Library of Congress Control Number: 2015941986

Cataloging-in-Publication Data

Murray, Julie.

 Arms & hands / Julie Murray.

   p. cm. -- (Your body)

ISBN 978-1-68080-156-9 (lib. bdg.)

Includes index.

1. Arm--Juvenile literature. 2. Hand--Juvenile literature.   I. Title.

612/.97--dc23

                        2015941986

Table of Contents

Arms and Hands. 4

Parts of the
Arm & Hand 22

Glossary. 23

Index 24

Abdo Kids Code. 24

Arms and Hands

Arms are part of your body.

You have two arms.

You lift things with your arms. Will lifts the box.

Arms **bend** at the elbows.

Hands are part of your body.

You have two hands.

Each hand has five fingers.

You have ten fingers!

You touch with your hands.

Molly touches the bunny.

You pick things up with your hands. Al picks up the ball.

Arms and hands work together.

Joe waves to his friend.

Some animals have arms and hands. A gorilla has long arms. It has big hands!

Parts of the Arm & Hand

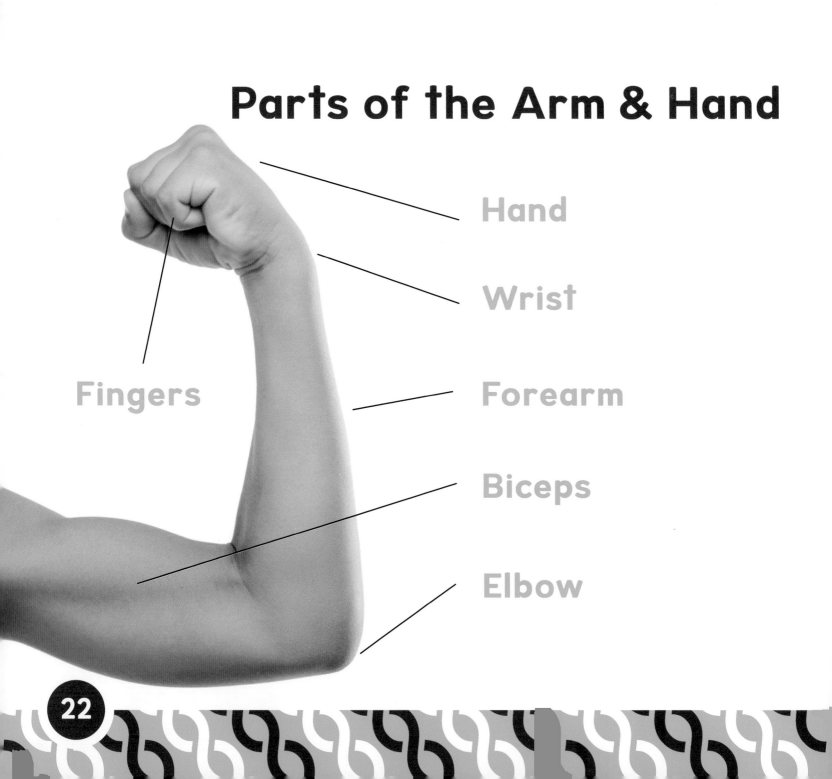

Hand

Wrist

Fingers

Forearm

Biceps

Elbow

Glossary

bend
move from straight to angled.

lift
pick up.

Index

arm 4, 6, 8, 18, 20

elbow 8

finger 12

gorilla 20

hand 10, 12, 14, 16, 18, 20

lift 6

touch 14

wave 18

abdokids.com

Use this code to log on to abdokids.com and access crafts, games, videos, and more!

Abdo Kids Code:

YAK1569